Fennec Fox as a Pet

Pet

The Complete Owner's Guide

Fennec Fox facts, habitat, care, price, breeders, training, laws, diet, cost, health, all covered!

Copyright and Trademarks

Disclaimer and Legal Notice

produce any particular results and the advice and strategies, contained herein may not be suitable for every individual. The author shall not be liable for any loss incurred as a consequence of the use and application, directly or indirectly, of any information presented in this work. This publication is designed to provide information in regard to the subject matter covered.

Acknowledgement

I fully dedicate this book to my loving husband;
Who showered me in his never ending support,
Who gave me inspiration and encouragement—
Words cannot express how much you mean to me
And how thankful I am
For having you as my hubby and my friend.

Table of Contents

Table of Contents

Table of Contents

Table of Contents

Table of Contents

Chapter 1. What are Fennec Foxes

The fennec fox, though known scientifically as *Vulpes zerda*, received its name Fennec from the Arabic word "fanak", which means fox. With their loveable large ears and small bodies, they are quite adorable little foxes, which make them highly attractive to prospective pet owners.

Fennec foxes have varying names. A male fox is called a reynard, a female fox is called a vixen, and a baby fennec fox is referred to as a cub, pup, or a kit. A group of foxes are termed as a leash or skulk.

Chapter 1. What are Fennec Foxes

The fennec fox, or simply a fennec, is a tiny fox that is nocturnal, which means the fox is awake and more active during night time.

The number one distinguishable feature of fennecs is its huge and bat-like ears relative to its small body size. Fennecs are known to be the smallest species of fox and canid in the whole world. (Canidae or canid is a biological terminology use to refer to a group of coyotes, jackals, foxes, wolves, domestic dogs and some extinct species that are dog-like mammals.)

Fennec foxes are found mainly from the Saharan Desert of North Africa to the Arabian Peninsula. Their habitats comprise mainly of arid, hot days, and cold nights with low water environments. They are burrowers and are very agile. Like any depiction of the fox animal as a whole, they are wise and witty.

Living in the Desert where there is little to no source of water, fennecs are well adapted to their habitat in that they can subsist for long periods without water.

A. Physical Description of Fennec Fox

Since fennec foxes belong to the biological classification of Canidae, it shares several characteristics with its close relatives like the coyotes, jackals, foxes, wolves, and domestic dogs among many others.

Chapter 1. What are Fennec Foxes

Fennecs, just like other canids, possess non-retractile claws and bushy tails. Further, like all canids they are digitrade, which means that they walk on their toes. They also have a dewclaw which is the human equivalent of a thumb or almost always denoted as a dog's thumb, which never comes into contact with the floor whenever canids are standing.

a. Weight And Height

As we have said earlier, fennec foxes are the smallest canid in the world. Its average weight as an adult is between 2-3.5 lbs. (0.91 to 1.6 kilograms). Its body's average length is between 9 to 16 inches long (23 to 41 cm), and its average height is around 8 inches tall (20 cm). The tails of fennecs are also long with an average length of 7 to 12 inches (18 to 31 cm). Also, the fennec's bat-like ears averages between 3.5 to 6 inches long (9 – 15 cm).

b. Coloration

Fennec foxes have a fawn or cream colored fur coat which is soft and fluffy, while the belly is covered in creamy white fur. Their cream colored fur helps them to blend in perfectly with the desert sand, so they are great at hiding. In reality, the fennec's fur is well sought after by indigenous North African tribes and other parts of the Earth. Their tails are also cream colored and the tips of their tails are black. The soles of fennec's paw are also furred and the anal gland is all covered with dark bristles.

c. Locomotor Skills

Fennec foxes are very agile animals and can dart easily from one sand dune to another or back and forth. Running at high speeds of up to 20 mph, fennecs also have the uncanny ability to change directions quickly. Another skill that these creatures have is the ability to jump up as high as two feet and they can lunge forward as long as four feet away. They are also extremely skillful at digging holes and can dig up a hole up to a length of 20 feet in just one night!

B. Taxonomy

When naming and classifying fennec foxes, scientists are at a loss because there are several characteristics that fennecs exhibit that is against the usual traits of a fox. Such differing characteristics of fennecs are not only physical but also social. This has led to the naming confusion in the scientific scene.

Among the physical differences between other foxes and the fennec is that the latter only has 32 pairs of chromosome in its DNA, whilst other foxes have 39 and 35 pairs. Further, social behaviors of fennecs like living in packs is the opposite for other foxes' social life who prefer to live solitary lifestyles.

Some scientists say that because of these differing characteristics, the fennec should have a genus of its own which they identified as *Fennecus,* (hence the old scientific name of fennecs as *Fennecus zerda)*. However, a new classification prevailed and this classified fennecs along with other foxes under the genus *Vulpes*.

a. Scientific Classification

Kingdom: Animalia
Phylum: Chordata
Class: Mammalia
Order: Carnivora
Family: Canidae
Genus: Vulpes (Fox)
Species: Zerda (Arabic for Fennec, Meaning Small)

Common Name: Fennec Fox
Scientific Name: *Vulpes zerda*

C. Evolution and Adaptation

The fennec fox is a highly evolved and well adapted animal that can live in the harsh conditions of the desert. Several physical adaptations of the fox help it move around, subsist, and generally live a good long life in the desert. Likewise, they are well-adapted to the desert environment with regards to their lifestyle, behavior, and capability.

a. Physical Adaptations

The fennec's light colored fur helps in deflecting heat during the day and helps protect them from the cold nights of the desert. Also, they have thick fur which helps deflect either the cold or the heat.

Their paws are well padded and have long soft fur too. This enables them to walk on the hot sands of the desert and provides traction—making them agile even on sand. Likewise the fur also acts as snowshoes which enable them to walk on snow without sinking. Their paws are also well adapted to digging which helps them to create burrows under the ground or make escape routes in the sand.

Their strong hind legs allow them to jump off the ground up to heights of two feet to a meter which enables them to reach for food or prey above ground. The ability to lunge four feet away also helps them in catching food or evading prey. Plus, their uncanny ability to dig fast and burrow helps them create a livable house in the desert or to hide quickly from predators.

Its long and bat-like ears are among its highly adapted characteristics. Their ears are very sensitive and allow fennecs to hear their prey located above the ground and even under the ground! Their long bat ears also contain plenty of blood vessels which help them to radiate heat and keep themselves cool in the searing hotness of the desert. Hairs within their inner ears prevent the entry of insects and sands within.

Fennec foxes also have a highly evolved retina called a tapetum, which gives them a much improved night vision for them to hunt successfully at night. This reflective retina gives the illusion of glowing eyes —a characteristic shared between nocturnal animals.

Lastly, their capability to subsist on very little water is extremely helpful in the desert environment. Its kidneys are another highly adapted physical characteristic of the fennec, which enables it to conserve water and excrete highly concentrated urine. They have the mysterious ability to get their water needs from the foods they have eaten thus enabling them to go on for long periods without drinking water.

b. Behavioral and Lifestyle Adaptations

Fennec foxes begin to shiver with cold when the temperature drops below 68° F (20°C). However, they only begin to overheat at high temperatures starting at around 105° F (40°C). When fennecs begin to overheat they pant in order to dissipate body heat and maintain normal temperatures within the body.

Chapter 1. What are Fennec Foxes

In normal conditions a fennec fox's breathing rate averages 23 breaths per minute. However, when they overheat their breathing rate can go as fast as 690 breaths per minute which is a very astonishing rate — this only goes to show that they are very well-adapted to desert conditions. Another survival adaptation that fennec foxes have is their ability to produce a number of litters that depends on the abundance of food supply. Normally, they produce only one litter per year. However, when all pups die or there is substantial source of food, fennec foxes can produce another litter for that year ensuring the family's numbers.

Another lifestyle adaptation of these fennecs is the behavior of storing their excess food under the ground for future consumption.

Lastly, their nocturnal behavior protects the fennec from the extreme heat of the midday sun, which enables them to make the most out of their habitat at night and rest during daytime.

Chapter 2. Understanding Fennec Foxes (In the Wild)

If you are interested in purchasing a fennec fox as a pet, or even the current owner of a fennec fox, then it is to you and your pet's advantage that you learn more about them. It's helpful to learn about their natural environment and how they react within, as well as their communication style, behavior, their social systems in place, and their life span. By understanding the natural ways of your pet, you get a better understanding of their behavior and the reasons behind their activities.

You may be baffled or angry about your fennec fox's way of constantly digging on your floor, or by the high screeched noises that it may make at times, and so on. But instead of getting angry or worse hurting your pet for something that is in its nature, the best recourse is for you is to understand your fennec.

As a pet owner, it is no mean feat taking care of these little adorable creatures. They require patience, effort, and understanding. And in return for that, your pet also gives you happiness and satisfaction. So, here is a bit more information to begin your journey of understanding your pet fennec.

Chapter 2. Understanding Fennec Foxes

A. Behavior

Fennec foxes are very energetic animals. They can dart from place to place and they love to dig. They have a tremendous appetite for digging and can dig holes and burrows of 20 feet long in just one night. They can jump up to a height of two feet and lunge up to four feet forward in order to catch prey or elude a predator.

Their agility enables them to change course in the middle of a speedy chase or while running. With this energy and stamina, fennecs in the wild are also observed to engage in play.

Fennecs are bright little creatures that keep or stash their excess foods in holes or burrows which they can return to after several days or months. And the amazing thing is that, they do remember where the stash is located from season to season.

They are territorial animals and mark their territories with their scent through urine and piles of their very own feces. They are also spirited defenders of their territory and pups. However, fennec foxes are social animals and live in groups of up to ten individuals. Within a group it is noticed that dominant males tend to urinate more at marking sites than other non-dominant male of the group.

During mating, fennecs mate with only one partner for life. The mother fennec attends to the babies for the first two weeks of the babies' life and most often the father is not allowed in the den and is just outside guarding it during that time.

Both the mom and the dad fennec work together to rear their young until six months of age, but even then the litter can stay within the group and help in rearing the next batch of litters.

Fennecs dig burrows as their den or home where they can rear their children. These burrows are usually created underneath desert bushes so that the roots of these plants give support to the burrows. Sometimes, these burrows can have more than one exit and entrance and can even become a maze-like structure that also connects to other groups of fennec fox's burrow. A fennec's burrow/den can be larger than a football field!

Though fennec foxes have a big social group, when they go hunting they do this solitarily. And since they are nocturnal, they only hunt at night.

B. Communication

Fennec foxes make several different calls or sounds that can mean different things depending on the situation. Since, there is not much study on fennec foxes in the wild, the sounds and calls mentioned in this part is basically coming from pet owners' observation.

Fennecs make low guttural barking sounds which mean that they are feeling threatened or upset. When they do this it is best not to approach the fennec. But, if your fennec pet is well cared for and content, rarely do they make this type of barking noise.

Another sound that typifies an angry fennec is a cross between a growl and purr. When they make this sound, the fennec may want to be left alone, so give it space. According to pet owners, pet fennecs exhibit this type of growling purr sound when they are being held in the owner's arms and want to be put down.

Male fennecs also make a deeper chirping trill in the wild which is commonly recorded. This is usually made by male fennecs that are searching for mates and is thus called the mating call. However, neutered males (male animals that have their reproductive organs removed), do not exhibit this type of call or sound.

Fennecs also make a happy sound, much like a very high squealing noise and also wag their tails like dogs. This means that they are delighted to see their pet owner, excited, and/or they want to be petted.

C. Reproduction

There is little literature that studies how fennecs choose a mate in the wild and even in captivity. But, one thing is for sure, fennec foxes are monogamous in nature and are cooperative breeders.

Cooperative breeding is a social arrangement where members of the group provide care for the young aside from the care given to the offspring by the breeding and dominant parent in the group. This increases survival rate for all members of the group through sharing of work.

a. Breeding Facts

Fennecs breed only once every year. However, there is an exception to this rule of thumb when and if all kits in the litter die and/or there is abundant source of food for that season, the dominant male and female fennec can breed and create a second litter.

Chapter 2. Understanding Fennec Foxes

The breeding season starts in January and ends in February. After 50 to 53 days of gestation, the mother fennec gives live birth to a litter of kits. So pups are born between the months of March and April.

The number of pups in a litter is also dependent on environmental conditions, wherein low source of food will yield a low number of pups and abundant food will yield a high number of kits. In a litter the number of offspring is usually between two to five kits.

The mother fennec lactates for a span of nine to ten weeks, which is just right because kits are weaned starting at 30 to 90 days from when they were born.

b. Reproductive Maturity

Male fennecs reach reproductive maturity earlier, on average, than their female counterparts. The males are able to reproduce six to nine months from its birth, while female fennecs reach full sexual maturity between six to eleven months after birth. Further, full sexual maturity of kits, whether male or female, is reached when the kits also reach their full adult size.

c. Copulation

Similar to other canids, fennec foxes often experience the copulatory tie during the second stage of mating. This locks their genitals together for minutes or even a couple hours at a time while faced in the opposite direction. After mating, the male fennec becomes quite protective of its mate and aggressive towards strangers which he deems poses a threat to his mate.

D. Child rearing

Fennecs rear their children with the help of other members of the group. From the time kits are born, the father and any other adult male in the group are not allowed to enter the den and come near the kits. The fennec is vicious and aggressive during this stage and will guard her litter with her life.

a. Kits Upon Birth

Upon birth, each kit on average weighs 26.28 grams or barely an ounce. Their eyes are shut and somewhat sealed. Their ears are bent over just like the ears of domestic dogs. These kits are swathed in light peach fur. Their skin is colored grey and if it contains dark markings these will also come out in their fur when they become adults.

They are nursed by their mother within an underground burrow. During this time, the dominant male fennec provides the mother with food to sustain her—this is also done when the female is undergoing gestation and lactation periods.

b. Kits Transformation to Adult

The kits' eyes open between 12 to 14 days from its birth. Their little ears start to stand erect around two weeks of age. During this time, the kits ears exhibit a notable growth pattern and changes are measurably obvious daily. In a short span of time, the kits with their young bodies already have full grown fennec fox ears.

At four weeks old, the kits begin to play within the den and on the fifth week play can extend near the exit of the den. During this time, kits can now exit the den and stay near its entrance but not really leaving it totally.

This is also the time when the mother allows the kits to interact with their father. The kits are closely watched, carried and licked by the mother, father, and sometimes other group members for up to 10 weeks of age.

Only at three months old are the kits allowed to leave the den and it is around this time that they are weaned from suckling from their mom. And only at six to nine months after birth have fennec kits achieved full independence.

E. Social System

The fennec fox's basic social unit is primarily composed of the dominant male and his mate. Then they are joined by their litter of kits and their previous litter which are now adults. This is mainly based on captive bred fennec foxes. However, in the wild, they cannot properly identify if all members of the group are related or unrelated to one another.

Since their system is built around cooperative breeding, the reproductive success of all sexually mature adults in the skulk is repressed—meaning they are not able to breed. Only the dominant male of the skulk is able to reproduce with its partner.

For the dominant pair, this is very beneficial because they have helping hands to help bring up their kits and added members to help defend the den. For non-sexually reproductive members of the skulk, this gives them benefits too by giving them more time to hunt for food and more protection because of the skulk's numbers.

F. Life span

The life span of fennec foxes in the wild is between ten to twelve years. However, in captivity, fennec foxes exhibit a longer life span of 11 to 14 years.

Chapter 3. Fennec Fox Habitat

In order to provide your current or future fennec fox pet with the right lodging, food, and care it is of equal importance to know these creatures' native habitat. This is because most of their adaptations physically—and behaviorally as well, are much attuned with their habitat.

Further, when you know more about your fennec's natural habitat you can help give them their close to normal housing, food, and care.

A. Geographic Range

Fennec foxes live in the dry arid lands and the deserts of Asia and North Africa. This landscape extends from Egypt to Morocco and as far east as Kuwait and the Sinai Peninsula and as far north as Niger.

However due to the pet trade, fennecs are now found within domestic households from the USA and Europe. They are also kept in captivity in certain zoos as part of their wildlife preservation and for part of research and studies.

a. Climate Conditions

The climate conditions of half the geographic range of the fennec foxes only have an inch of rain annually, especially within the central Sahara Desert. However on other regions rainfall can reach up to four inches each year. But, these rains pour torrentially and are not spaced out all throughout the year.

The Sahara Deseret has the most unforgiving climate in the whole world. As we all know the Sahara is an extremely hot region with an average temperature of 86°F (30°C) during the day. However, throughout the hottest times of the year the temperature could surpass 130°F (54°C).

After sunset, because the desert has no clouds and the air is so dry, the temperature drops suddenly. The temperature difference between day and night could be as high as 50°F (28°C). In other words, an average temperature at night would be 36°F (2°C), compared to 86°F (30°C) during the day —from melting hot to nearly freezing cold temperatures.

During winter time it is also known that overnight freezes are common and snowfall does occur in the desert region but it dissipates quickly.

b. Topography

The Sahara Desert is not solely made of sand dunes and sand ergs. But a large portion of the Sahara Desert is made up of rocky Hamada, which is a typical desert landscape primarily made up of rocky, hard and barren plateaus— where there is little to no sand.

The Sahara Desert may contain some rivers and streams but their presence is just seasonal; aside from the Nile River which has a permanent presence.

Within the central portion of the Sahara there is much reduced plant growth. But on the Southern and Northern edges of the Sahara and including the highlands, there is vegetation although it is quite sparse—but enough to sustain a few animals like the fennecs, rats, mice, hyenas, and more.

Examples of vegetation that grow here are desert shrubs, grassland, and sometimes there are taller shrubs and trees—where moisture can collect.

B. Habitat Conditions

The fennec's ideal habitation is the sand dunes where they create burrows. Ideally, stable sand dunes are much preferred because of its compacted soils which create a stable structure for their dens.

Within this type of substrate, dens of fennecs can form elaborate tunnels underneath with plenty of exits and entrances. Further, these mazes of tunnels and dens can interconnect with other fennec groups' dens or are located nearby.

However, fennecs still use looser sand dunes as a substrate for their dens. Dens within this kind of habitat are usually simpler with only one chamber and one tunnel that serve both as an entryway and exit.

The fennecs' burrows or den chambers are padded with soft materials like feathers, bits of fur, and leaves to make the place comfortable.

a. Desert Flora or Vegetation

Most of the Saharan desert plants are well adapted to the region's dryness, excessive heat, and unreliable precipitation. These plants are an important source of food, housing structure, water, and livelihood for desert animals—the fennec fox included. Sahara is home to widely scattered vegetation like grasses, shrubs, herbs, succulents and trees.

Grasses

The most common grass species in the Saharan desert are the aristida, panicum, and eragrostis. The panicum grass survives in the desert by growing independently rather than in clumps which gives it better capacity to make use of the water or nutrients within an area. It is used for thatch, fodder, and flour. The eragrostis or lovegrass is a fast growing plant and is widespread in the desert.

Herbs

One of the herbs that grow in the Saharan Desert is the Thyme. It is drought resistant and is a major food source.

Shrubs

Among the shrubs of the desert are the papyrus sedge, Mormon tea plant, and the Ephedra. The sedge typically grows near the Nile River while Ephedra is widely spread in the desert. It bears berry like cones or fruits which desert animals eat.

Succulents

Succulents are desert plants that have the capability to retain water within their bodies—thus the term succulent or juicy. Examples of these are the Peyote cactus, desert lily, golden barrel cactus, and the African welwitchsia. The latter is also well known for its capability to grow its roots far down into the earth in order to get water, which allows it to survive in the desert for hundreds of years.

Trees

There are trees that grow in the Saharan desert and these are magaria trees, olive trees, doum palms, common fig, red acacia, Joshua trees, and date palms. These trees provide food and shelter for the desert animals.

b. Desert Fauna or Animals

There are quite a handful of desert animals, but we will be focusing only on the animals that are important to fennec foxes as a whole and these are mainly its predators and its food sources. Samples of these desert animals are birds, reptiles, insects, small rodents, and small mammals.

It's important to note too that most desert animals are nocturnal as an adaptation mechanism against the severe heat of the sun. While others may not be nocturnal, they usually hide from the mid-day sun and are likely to be up and about during dusk and dawn.

Birds

Among the desert's birds are the flightless ostrich which makes up for its fast running skills for its inability to fly. It also lays huge eggs and is mostly found near watering holes of the desert. Ostrich eggs are an important source of food for fennecs in the wild.

Other birds in the desert are: black faced finch, African Silverbill, Nubian Bustard, the red-tailed hawk, pigeons, brown-necked ravens, and many other migratory birds that also lay eggs in the desert.

The Desert Eagle Owl is primarily the best known predator of the fennec, which also lays eggs in the desert. However, fennecs prey on small birds for food themselves.

Rodents

There are plenty of rodents that live in the Saharan desert amounting to as much as 40 different species. Among the many species are: banner tailed kangaroo rat, jerboa, gerbils, and others. Again, these animals also forms part of the fennec diet.

Small Mammals

There are also small mammals that abound in the Saharan desert on which fennecs prey on like the hyrax, which looks like a rodent but is actually more related to elephants. Other small mammals are mongoose, badgers, hedgehogs, weasels, and others. These are also part of the fennec's diet in the wild.

Insects

Insects are perhaps the most widespread of animals and are therefore present in the Saharan Desert under the following forms: dung beetles, ants, locusts, scarab beetles, spiders, moths, dragonflies, flies, and leaf bugs to name a few. These are amongst the fennec's diet in the desert.

Reptiles

Samples of reptiles in the Saharan desert are snakes, lizards, and chameleons to name a few. These small reptiles form part of the fennec's diet in the wild.

C. Diet and Feeding Habits

The fennec fox is an omnivore, which means its diet consists of meat and plants. They eat whatever is available from insects to lizards, eggs, birds, mice, grass, berries, and fruits.

They also eat carrions which are left over meat of bigger desert predators.

a. Meat Diet

Among the fennecs' meat diet are mice, lizards, small birds, and insects. Fennecs are great hunters because of their acute sense of hearing. When hunting for food they seem to stare at the sand and rotate their heads from side to side.

This gives the fennec a clear location of their prey below the ground. Combine their keen sense of hearing with their superb digging habit, and what you get is equal to a precision killing machine—their prey never knows what hits it.

Above the ground, fennecs are also well equipped in hunting their prey. Their sharp hearing allows them to easily track their prey. Their padded paws which can muffle their steps, their excellent night vision, and their ability to lunge a meter away makes them an efficient desert hunter.

b. Plant Diet

Fennecs also eat plants like berries, fruits, roots, and grasses. This part of their diet helps them get water or moisture, especially in the desert where there is little to no water source. Their capability to eat plants allows them to survive without water for long periods of time.

c. Water Source

Though fennecs are well-adapted to not drinking water for long periods of time, we still have to note that they do and can drink water directly. Aside from getting a portion of their water needs from plants, fennecs' kidneys are also well adapted such that it helps in regulating the body to restrict water loss.

Another adaptation for conserving body fluid is by producing very concentrated urine. Further, the fennecs' burrowing can produce dew formation which they can drink, although it's just a few licks.

d. Feeding Habits

Just like any old fox's tales, fennecs are wise little rascals. They store excess foods in their dens. They are also known to stow their excess foods by storing it in other underground places and they have the memory to return to it even after seasons or months' have passed.

Fennecs are known as opportunistic feeders which mean that they eat whatever makes itself available from insects, to lizards, birds, eggs and rodents.

e. Kit Feeding Habit

Kits in the wild are normally fed mother's milk until they are a month old. However, many fennec foxes feed longer than others and full weaning may not occur until 3 months of age. In the process of weaning they have a mixed diet of milk and regurgitated meat which the vixen has eaten for the kits.

After a while, the kits are allowed aside the den where the mother or father brings back a live prey like mice or insects wherein the kits are taught how to kill the prey. Soon they are allowed to go with the parent on a hunting occasion and are then formally taught how to hunt. Eventually the kits are also taught how to store excess food.

Chapter 3. Fennec Fox Habitat

D. Predators

The number one predator of fennecs is the different
varieties of African Eagle Owls. These bird species are
nocturnal, just like fennecs. Although, the hearing of
fennecs are quite keen, the owl is also a ruthless and silent
killer that almost always gives no hint of its presence,
descent, and approach to its prey.

Other reports say that wild dogs, saluki, hyenas, jackals,
and caracals are also predators of fennecs however there is
much debate about this because fennecs have a keen sense
of hearing. Miles away it can already detect the approach of
the said predators which would give it plenty of time to
escape or burrow and hide. Anyway, it has been decided
that this needs further study in order to be considered as
true.

E. Threats to Habitat

Currently, due to human settlement expansion there are
reported cases wherein fennecs' habitat and entire
population of fennecs have disappeared. One such place is
in Southern Morocco.

F. Relationship with other animals in the habitat

It seems that fennecs have no known relationship or
positive relationship with other animals in the desert

environment because it eats whatever it sees. It is a highly private animal and because of its acute hearing, it can go into hiding right away. Therefore, further studies are needed to prove otherwise.

Chapter 4. Fennec Fox Conservation

Fennec Fox Conservation is guided by several factors. Almost always, animals that are rigorously protected are the ones with a severely declining population or only have a handful of individuals left in the wild or in captivity like zoos and wildlife preserves.

In this chapter, you get to learn the conservation practices or codes that are applicable to fennec populations in the wild. You also get to learn if their populations are on a decline and if it is, why it is so.

A. Ecosystem Roles

As a desert predator, fennecs are valuable animals that help in curbing the population growth of small mammals, birds, reptiles, and insects. Without them, it could lead to ecosystem instability, like overgrowth of insects and rodents.

This could cause the demise of other animal populations within the desert and the growth of a dominant few. This is what an ecosystem imbalance would look like. It may not be felt or seen right away but it is highly probable as evidenced by other imbalanced ecosystems in the world.

Chapter 4. Fennec Fox Conservation

Fennecs' habit of lining their den of vegetation and eating plants as well—are not detrimental to the plant population as evidenced by a study conducted by Estes in 1991.

B. Economic Importance to Humans

Saharan natives find the fennec to be very important. Unfortunately however, not for what many would consider ethical reasons. They often hunt fennecs for their soft fur.

Aside from that, fennecs are of importance to humans because they are becoming more popular as pets, and also as features in zoos. In terms of a negative impact to humans, there is no known negative impact to humans caused by fennecs.

C. IUCN Status

IUCN stands for International Union for Conservation of Nature. They are the largest and oldest global environmental organization, which helps in preserving earth's biodiversity.

According to IUCN Red List—a comprehensive, objective and global analysis on the threats, trends, and status of a species—the fennecs are Data Deficient.

This means that further studies on population in the wild needs to be done in order to form a definitive scenario of its population count and threats to its existence. Also, according to IUCN it is a Least Concern species when it comes to conservation efforts.

D. Current Population

There are no sources available that lists the current fennec fox population number in the wild. However, there are some concerns about population decline in certain areas.

E. Threats To Fennec Fox Population

As reported earlier, the fennec population may be a concern in certain areas because of human encroachment to their habitat. It has even been reported in Southern Morocco that populations of fennecs have completely disappeared from the area due to establishment of new and permanent settlements near the fennecs' habitat.

As mentioned earlier, another threat to fennec population is from sport hunters and being hunted by native Saharan people because of their prized fur within the tribe's culture. Fennecs are also trapped to be sold to tourists.

It should be noted, that in the USA, most fennec foxes are sold by USDA certified breeders who have *not* obtained their foxes from the wild. They have been bred in the USA as pets since the 1970's. This does not contribute to a potential fennec fox population issue. In fact, fennec foxes live a longer and safer live in captivity when cared for properly.

F. Conservation Efforts

Currently, there are no international conservation efforts for fennec foxes. However, in Morocco—including Western Sahara, Egypt, Tunisia, and Algeria, fennecs are already legally protected.

Fennecs are also listed in CITES – Appendix II for the following protected areas: Tunisia, Niger, Mauritania, Libya, Egypt and Algeria.

Being listed in CITES – Appendix II would mean that: fennecs are not essentially currently in peril of extinction but that they may become so if only trade is closely regulated. International trade of fennecs may be approved by the giving of a re-export certificate or export permit. Certificates or Permits should only be given if the appropriate officials are satisfied that definite criteria are met; above all that, trade must not be harmful to the persistence of the fennecs in the wild.

Chapter 5. What to Know Before You Buy

As a prospective buyer of fennecs foxes, here is a basic list of what you need to know in order to make a good decision about if you are ready to be an owner. This chapter will ready you on the many issues and benefits of owning a fennec. It will ready you on the general guidelines in order to own one legally. It will also inform you in no uncertain terms on the rigorous job of taking care of one.

Of course, we will also inform you on the many advantages that owning a fennec can bring to your life. Lastly, once you know all there is to know about owning one; we leave the decision making to you. As a pet owner too, I hope that you will make the right decision that would benefit both you and your pet fennec.

Further, the USDA only allows buying of fennecs from USDA certified breeders. No fennecs should be bought or taken from the wild. Lastly, no fennecs should be bought beforehand without having the required permits (if applicable) from your state.

A. Covering the Basics

It is legal to own a fennec fox in many states in the US, but there are some who are apprehensive about it due to it being an exotic pet.

While there are some individuals who don't particularly like the idea of taking care of exotic pets, there are numerous pet owners who successfully take care of exotics, including fennec foxes.

Fennec foxes, are not domesticated thus they can be aggressive at times. For this reason, it is important for those who wish to take care of fennecs to always handle them with care.

It is also important to provide them with their basic needs. Additionally, because they are curious animals, it is important that they are regularly supervised. Thus only responsible pet owners should consider purchasing a fennec fox.

Chapter 5. What to Know Before You Buy

a. How many should I buy?

So, by now you have a better understanding of fennec foxes, but how many should you buy? In states where care for them is legal, , there are no laws that stipulate how many fennec foxes a pet owner is allowed to take care of (with the exception of one state, which will be discussed later).

Still, if you are a first time owner of a fennec fox, then it is best to purchase just one fennec fox so that you can focus on taking care of your pet, bonding with your pet, and learning its needs and behaviors. In time you can add another fennec fox to your family if you prefer, as adding a new pet member can be beneficial. Even so, be sure to consider your budget as well as the amount of time that you are willing to spend to care for your fox, especially before considering the purchase of another. Remember, fennec foxes live in groups in the wild so they normally don't mind the company of another fennec fox. However, it is best to get acquainted with just one first.

b. The Best Age of Fennec to Buy

Sometimes, prospective buyers don't give this important question a thought, but knowing the age of your fennec beforehand can make or break a deal.

Generally speaking, the younger the age of your fennec, the better it is for you as a pet owner because this would give you more time to bond and socialize with your pet. However, you can't purchase a fennec that is too young either, because it will need time to be weaned from drinking milk. So you should buy a fennec fox when the kit is between four to six weeks of age. This is around the time when the kit is weaned from the bottled milk and is also sufficient enough time for you to start bonding with your new pet. *Do* make sure that the fennec is weaned before purchasing so that you don't have to worry about bottle feeding. Leave that to the professionals.

It should also be noted that how your fennec fox was "raised" is equally important. It is essential that the fennec fox you purchase has been pulled to be bottle fed at around 2 weeks of age. A fennec fox that is parent raised rather than bottle-fed or pulled will not be as socialized and will likely be aggressive.

c. Know that Fennecs Cannot be Re-homed

Fennecs cannot be re-homed or sold all over again to different pet owners. Some fennecs may have a tendency to attach themselves to their first owners, thus the earlier you get acquainted with them, the better their disposition will be with you; as opposed to a fennec having several different owners which would bring out the worst of its temperament. It is very difficult to care for a fennec that has been rehomed.

Secondly, rehoming may make them distrust their new home and new owner, and ultimately it would no longer be pet quality.

Thirdly, foxes are not like pet dogs. They do not have the need or desire to please their pet owners—much less humans as a whole. So, that early bonding time is crucial.

And lastly, if this rehomed pet fennec thinks, feels, or perceives that a human has wronged it (presumably a previous pet owner) then it will likely go on thinking that way and will behave accordingly.

With that being said however, there are still some who choose to rehome fennecs. But they are very experienced individuals who provide the fennec with a great living situation, the proper care, and go the extra mile to bond with the rehomed fennec. This is usually done in order to save a fox that it is no longer wanted. While this is an incredibly kind gesture, it should not be taken on by someone who is inexperienced, let alone a first time fennec fox owner.

d. Advantages of Owning Fennec Foxes

There are many benefits to owning an exotic animal like the fennec fox. This small member of the canine family gives much joy to their pet owners. Below are some of the advantages of taking care of fennec foxes as pets.

- Since fennec foxes are so small, they are quite desired, and loveable. They are great conversation pieces especially if you have visitors in your home.

- These cute canines live up to 16 years in captivity thus pet owners can build a long lasting bond between their pets.

- Fennec foxes are highly energetic and playful animals so there's never a dull day. They are very intriguing and you can watch them run around and play for hours, as well as join in on the fun and play with them.

- Unlike many other foxes, fennec foxes have virtually no foul body odor (unless they are afraid in which case they will release a smell similar to a skunk). However, the smell doesn't linger much or last long.

- Similar to cats, fennec foxes clean themselves so they require very minimum care where hygiene is concerned. As long as your fennec doesn't get into a huge mess, you will not need to bathe it regularly. Fennecs also do not shed much fur.

- They provide love, entertainment, excitement, and enjoyment for many of their pet owners.

e. Disadvantages of Owning Fennec Foxes

Though fennec fox owners love caring for their fennecs, it is also important to understand that since they are originally wild animals, they have retained some of their natural instincts. In fact, there are some disadvantages of taking care of fennec foxes as you will see below.

- Fennec foxes are hyperactive animals so it is important that you keep an eye on them as much as possible. In fact, they are dubbed as "escape artists" in the desert because of their ability to evade their predators due to their digging skills and the ability to fit in tight spaces. For this reason, if you have a very busy home where people are often coming in and out, this might not be a good pet for you. A fennec fox will run off in seconds if given the opportunity. Also understand that once they escape, it's hard to find them—ever.

Chapter 5. What to Know Before You Buy

- Fennec foxes are difficult to litter train, so expect to see surprises everywhere in the house. Fennec foxes will go at any time. Often they won't even stop playing to relieve themselves. Usually when they have to go, they just go. For this reason, it is not recommended that you purchase a fennec fox if you have carpet in your home, or if the thought of finding surprises bothers you. On the bright side, their poop is usually stiff and firm, so it's easy to clean up.

- If you haven't tamed and bonded with your fennec fox early on when it is a kit, then it can become mean and aggressive and have the tendency to bite. Keep in mind that even if raised properly it still may nip, if it doesn't want to be bothered.

- Fennec foxes can be very loud. They make very high squealing and screeching noises when they are excited.

- Fennec foxes can be very destructive. They love to dig. They will dig at your carpet, hardwood floors, furniture, and at the walls. This is one of the many reasons why it is not recommended that you own a fennec fox if you are renting. There are certain things you can do to help with this issue (which will be discussed later), but you will never be able to stop it from digging completely. It is a natural instinct.

- You will need to find an exotic veterinarian who is willing and also experienced in treating a fennec fox, which can be a difficult task. You will also have to pay more for vet bills due to your fennec fox being an exotic animal.

- A fennec fox in combination with smaller pets in a home is not a good idea. If a fennec fox sees a smaller animal, its animal instincts will kick into high gear, and it will attempt to devour it. You will have to take precautionary measures to ensure your other smaller pets are safe.

- Fennec foxes are small and fragile, so they should be handled with the upmost care. You will also need to watch your step because they are quick and if you're not careful you could accidently step on your pet.

- Fennec foxes aren't super affectionate and don't like to be held for too long. They're pretty skittish. They will come to you when they want to, but usually they would rather be running around and playing.

- Unless in their cage or enclosure, fennec foxes should be supervised. They can get into all sorts of things and may cause harm to themselves or damage to your things if not supervised. You will have to fox-proof your home.

- Seeing as the only time they do not need supervision is when they are in their cage or enclosure, caring for a fennec fox can be time consuming. You need to not only look after your small fox, but to spend much time bonding with your pet as well.

- The care of fennec foxes requires more money than the everyday pet. Since they are omnivorous animals, feeding them with cat or dog food is not enough. Pet owners should also supply them with vegetables, insects, and other treats to supplement their diet. You will also need to pay for a cage, health expenses, and miscellaneous items.

- Not all fennec foxes are made equal. Some fennecs love everyone they meet, while other fennecs will only attach their selves to one individual and are very shy (this has a lot to do with how well they were socialized as well).

B. Legalizing Ownership

Anyone wishing to own a fennec fox must understand that it is absolutely vital to establish the requirements and legalities of doing so before purchasing the fox.

US residents should abide by all rules and laws regarding the care of fennecs. In the US, different states have different regulations regarding the care of such animals.

On the other hand, other countries such as the UK as well as most European countries seem to be lax about regulating the care of this exotic animal.

Below is an in-depth discussion on legalizing ownership of fennec foxes in both the US and the UK.

a. USA

Many states in the US do not require pet owners to get special permits or licenses to obtain fennec foxes as pets. Yet, there are still some states that prohibit the care, breeding, and sale of this particular animal. Here is a guide in legalizing ownership in the USA.

- Fennec foxes are legal in Arkansas, Kansas, New York, Ohio, Oklahoma, Michigan, Nebraska, Utah, Wisconsin, Tennessee, Pennsylvania, South Dakota, Rhode Island, and South Carolina.

- It is illegal to own fennec foxes as pets in Alabama, Alaska, California, Colorado, Virginia, New Mexico, New Hampshire, Connecticut, Washington, Oregon, Mississippi, Minnesota, Missouri, Nevada, New Jersey, Massachusetts, Hawaii, Kentucky, Idaho, Iowa, Georgia, Arizona, West Virginia, South Dakota, Vermont, Wyoming, and Texas.

- In Alabama, Delaware, Indiana, Illinois, Florida, Louisiana, Maine, Rhode Island, North Dakota and Nevada, pet owners can buy fennec foxes provided that they secure permits from the local animal control authority.

- There are states where fennecs are legal but on the condition that it comes with vet approbation. These states are: North Carolina, Montana.

- In Arkansas, it is unlawful to own more than six fennec foxes along with other medium-sized carnivores such as bobcats and coyotes.

- In Maryland, owning fennec foxes is banned but those who have owned fennec foxes before May 31, 2006 should make a written notification to the local animal control authority for record.

- In Wisconsin a fox must be kept in a pen (enclosure) at all times, that meets the minimum requirements as listed in the regulations pamphlet; a fox may not be kept in any part of a building or home where people live unless receiving temporary health care.

- In Pennsylvania you must have 2 years of experience, and an officer must come out to your home to inspect your enclosure (which must be bottom fenced with a shelf). You must also have a bill of sale and you are not allowed to purchase the fox until you receive your permit.

- <u>Warning!:</u> Although owning a fennec fox may be legal in your particular state, you must also check with your city and/or county, as exotic pet ownership can be regulated by any level of government. In other words, some individual cities/counties may prohibit the ownership of certain pets, even though the state allows it. This is not often the case, but it does happen. So *you* must ensure that you are following all state **and** county regulations in your area.

Furthermore, some states have very specific requirements in regards to enclosures. Some states also require that you have a bill of sale for the fox to serve as proof that you did not obtain the fox from the wild, but instead from a reputable breeder. Thus it is absolutely vital that you know what is expected before purchasing the fennec fox to confirm the legalities of owning one and to make yourself aware of any special requirements. This section is to serve as a <u>simple overview</u>. For the specific requirements of your area, please contact the Division of Wildlife or the Fish and Game department for your state, as well as the local animal ordinance for your city or county. Lastly, laws for exotic pets frequently change, so it is your responsibility to make sure that you are up to date, and that you are following the law at all times.

b. UK

Pet owners who want to own fennec foxes in the UK do not require special permits and licenses to own foxes. Although wild animals, pet owners are exempted from getting a dangerous wild animal's license at all.

C. Veterinarian

It is incredibly important that you find an **experienced** veterinarian <u>before</u> you purchase your fennec fox. You may need to call your vet, especially in the beginning stages, with any questions or concerns that you may have. Furthermore, in case there is an emergency and your fennec needs urgent care, you must already have a veterinarian in place.

It is important that you look for those who are qualified and licensed to work with fennec foxes. It is also important to note that they often charge more for their consultation for exotic animals. The location of the veterinarian may also be a factor, but I personally would rather travel a longer distance to an experienced fennec fox vet, than a shorter distance to a vet who is not so experienced. Obviously the closer they are the better, but be sure to take experience into consideration when choosing your veterinarian, as that is a huge factor. Finding the right vet who is experienced in taking care of fennec foxes is not an easy task compared with finding a vet for other common pets. However, once you have one in place you will feel more confident in being able to care of your pet properly.

a. Vaccines and Medications

Fennec foxes need preventative care similar to dogs, thus they can be given many similar shots as dogs. Currently there aren't any approved vaccines specifically for fennec foxes. However, it is very important that the vet *never* administers a live vaccine to your pet. <u>Killed and recombinant vaccines</u> are just fine. Even a modified live vaccine will suffice if a killed or recombinant vaccine is not available. But with their small bodies, administering **live** vaccines can be very dangerous to fennecs and will likely cause death as they will not be able to withstand the side effects. An experienced vet knows this fact but it still pays to inquire whether the vaccine that your vet will administer is a live one or not. Please remember, no live vaccines!

An important vaccine that you should get for your pet fennec fox is for canine distemper to help prevent mortality of your fennec fox. Distemper is a viral disease that can cause a fever and coughing, and affects the respiratory and central nervous system amongst other things. The typical MLV (modified live) vaccine for distemper should **not** be used for fennec foxes, as there is evidence that it may actually cause distemper rather than prevent it. Be absolute certain that your vet is aware of this. A safer vaccine for distemper will need to be administered.

Another vaccine that should be administered is the anti-rabies vaccine. This should help to put your mind at ease. Note: Although this vaccine will protect you and your fox from getting the disease, rabies vaccines are not proven effective for any other animals other than cats and dogs. So from a legal standpoint, if your fennec bites someone and they report it (because it is a fox), your pet could still be euthanized!

Like dogs, fennec foxes are also susceptible to parvovirus, which is a highly contagious illness (amongst dogs and fennecs, not humans), that causes diarrhea and vomiting. It can also be life threatening, thus a parvo vaccine is required. For parvo, a modified live vaccine will have to suffice as there aren't any killed or recombinant vaccines available for parvo.

It may also be necessary for vets to administer medications to fennec foxes to treat other health problems. For instance, fennecs are usually given Heartguard to prevent heartworms and/or a kitten dose of Revolution to prevent fleas. In any case, your veterinarian will advise what is best if that is necessary. For flea infestation, it is also important for pet owners to get shampoo and anti-flea products that is safe for small cats or kittens.

Overall, a yearly exam is recommended along with stool samples.

Note: Many USDA certified fennec fox breeders will include their necessary shots and health certificate with the purchase of the fox! Always ensure that the required vaccines have been administered and that you will receive a health certificate when you purchase your fennec fox if possible. From that point on, you should consult with your vet about how often vaccines will need to be administered going forward.

b. Other Health Concerns

Fennec foxes can be aggressive little animals at times, especially once they hit sexual maturity. Although it is not necessary, it is highly recommended to neuter your fox unless you are planning on breeding them (in which case you will need to obtain an USDA license). Spaying or neutering fennec foxes can help to curb their aggressive behaviors. If you plan on neutering your fennec fox, make sure that you do this procedure while they are about six to eight months old.

Your vet will need to put your pet under anesthesia but they must make sure that they are not given too much, as too much anesthesia can kill them. Fennecs should also be kept nice and warm at this time for comfort. Remember, fennec foxes are very fragile, thus they must be closely monitored.

Chapter 5. What to Know Before You Buy

c. Finding a Qualified Veterinarian

Taking care of your fennec fox means that you have to become a responsible pet owner, and part of being a responsible pet owner is finding a qualified vet. This could mean life or death for your pet.

Here are some websites that may assist in the search for exotic veterinarians:

http://www.localvets.com/ (USA)
http://www.aemv.org/   (USA and outside of USA)
http://www.vetworld.com   (USA and outside of USA)

* You must call the location to verify whether or not they have experience treating a fennec fox. Do not simply assume that every exotic veterinarian will be willing or have the experience to do so.

Chapter 10 may also be of assistance in locating a veterinarian. I list many helpful sites there about fennec foxes which may provide references on veterinarians that treat them. There is also a fennec fox forum listed in chapter 10 which will allow you to communicate with other fennec fox owners who may have info on experienced fennec fox vets in particular areas.

Chapter 6. Purchasing Fennec Foxes

Fennec foxes are becoming popular exotic pets due to their cute looks and playful nature. Although exotic, they are widely accepted in many places in the United States as well as other countries such as the UK. However, when purchasing them, it is important for would-be pet owners to know everything there is to know about purchasing pet fennec foxes from a reliable supplier.

When buying a pet fennec fox, there are some things that a pet owner should consider. One of the most important things that potential pet owners should know is how much fennec foxes cost. But not just the initial costs; the monthly costs as well. Below are guidelines on the price of owning and raising your very own fennec fox.

Chapter 6. Purchasing Fennec Foxes

A. Price of a Fennec Fox

The main reason fennec foxes are popular exotic pets is because they are small and incredibly cute. With their large ears and petite furry bodies, it is not difficult to fall in love with these small creatures.

However, most people are not aware of the costs associated with owning a fennec fox. The cost of the fennec fox itself will not be cheap. Also there are other costs that you need to shell out before you can own a fennec fox. For example you have to pay for permits if necessary, airfare for the pet if one must be shipped, and installation of their cages should be complete before you purchase one—especially in certain US states.

Below are some guidelines on how much money a pet owner should have in order to afford raising a pet fennec fox.

a. The Cost of Buying a Fennec Fox

Although small, fennec foxes are quite expensive. A young fennec fox – also called a kit – can cost between $1,000 and $3000 depending on the breeder, though $1500 is about average. Moreover, fennec foxes can be difficult to come by which is one of the main reasons why they are so expensive. You can't simply go to a pet store and purchase a fennec fox. For this reason, those who want to own fennec foxes as pets buy them directly from breeders.

Chapter 6. Purchasing Fennec Foxes

In the United States, there aren't a large number of licensed breeders that sell fennec foxes, and this is one of the biggest factors that affect the cost when purchasing a fennec fox.

Furthermore, fennec foxes that are bred by reliable and licensed breeders cost more because licensed breeders usually ensure that all of their fennec foxes are sanitized and free from disease. Further, fennec foxes that are bred by reliable breeders are usually already vaccinated and come with health certificates thereby making the task of getting a pet fennec fox all the more easier for the pet owner.

b. The Cost of Raising a Fennec Fox

Aside from shelling out a pretty penny upon the purchase of a fennec fox, pet owners also need funds to actually raise their fennec fox. Fennec fox owners must be prepared to spend money on food, shelter, healthcare, and other miscellaneous items.

c. Food Costs of Fennec Foxes

A fennec foxes' diet mainly consists of dog foods or cat foods in captivity, but it is equally important for pet owners to purchase other nourishments required by fennec foxes to provide a healthy and balanced diet. These pets are omnivorous thus their diets should not be limited to dog foods and cat foods.

Chapter 6. Purchasing Fennec Foxes

You will learn more about a fennec fox's diet in the next chapter, but when it comes to the food costs of fennec foxes, you will likely spend anywhere from $40-$60 (£25- £38) every month in order to provide the necessary nourishments that your pets need. This varies according to the type of diet you choose for your pet, they type of brands you choose, as well as your location.

d. Shelter Costs of Fennec Foxes

Fennec foxes are highly active animals especially during nighttime. Therefore, it is crucial for pet owners to provide them with the right shelter. Although it is not advised to cage fennec foxes all the time, they should be put into their enclosure when you are away from home for short periods of time, when you are unable to supervise them at particular periods of time, and at night time when you are sleeping. Thus, a cage/enclosure is absolutely necessary.

The cost of an inside enclosure for a fennec fox can range between $200 and $500 (£134.44 - £336.11) depending on the size and type. If you decide to purchase the cage that I recommend (which we will discuss in the next chapter), then about $250 (£157) will be sufficient.

e. Cost of Hygiene of Fennec Foxes

When it comes to their hygiene, pet owners of fennec foxes don't need to spend very much. Although fennec foxes do not litter train well, some owners still attempt litter training, in which case they would have to purchase the necessary products.

You will need to purchase a mild cat shampoo for when your fennec fox needs a bath, but since they do not need baths on a regular basis, that is not a purchase you will need to make too often.

You will need to purchase detergent to clean any blankets, hammocks, or other items that you fox may urinate on.

You may also want to buy certain cleaning products to aid in sanitizing and/or eliminating the smell of urine and feces, whether in the fennec foxes' cage or on your floor. The cost of hygiene for fennec foxes is estimated at $20-$30 (£13- £19) per month.

f. Cost of Healthcare of Fennec Foxes

Since fennec foxes are exotic animals, taking them to any veterinarian is not enough. You will need a veterinarian with experience handling fennec foxes. Since they are special pets, the cost of healthcare for fennec foxes is more expensive compared with that of cats and dogs. Moreover, pet owners also need to have money for any unexpected illnesses or conditions. The costs of healthcare for fennec foxes varies as veterinarians all have different rates. However, I recommend that you have a minimum of about $300 set aside for the first year of ownership. Once you have found an experienced fennec fox veterinarian it is best to speak with them about the exact pricing for visits, treatment, and the like, beforehand.

g. Miscellaneous Costs

In addition to food, shelter, hygiene, and healthcare costs, you will find that it is necessary to spend money on other items for your fennec as well. Some of these items include toys, blankets, a couple of pet beds or hammocks for its cage, food bowls, a collar and ID tag, permits if applicable, and a travel crate or pet carrier. Miscellaneous costs may cost between $100-200 (£67.22- £134.44). These are generally just one time purchases however.

It's always a good idea to put a little extra money aside before you purchase your fox.

B. Selecting a Breeder

Aside from the price, another important thing to consider when buying a fennec fox is the source of the animal. When buying fennec foxes, it is important that you buy from a reliable breeder. In the United States, breeders of fennec foxes should be regulated by the USDA.

Here are some of the things that you need to consider when choosing the right breeder for your fennec fox:

- The breeder should be duly licensed by the animal control authority. Ask for the breeders' USDA license number. Once you have the number you can click here or here to run a search to ensure it is valid. Or you can go to Google and type "USDA breeder search". The very first website listed should be that of the USDA search tool.

- Choose breeders that have years of experience in breeding fennec foxes. This is to ensure that the fennec fox that you are going to receive has been cared for by skilled individuals.

- Breeders should be knowledgeable when it comes to raising fennec foxes. Potential pet owners should not hesitate in asking questions about fennec foxes to breeders. In fact, many breeders will question *you* to ensure that you are ready for a fennec fox. This is a good sign; this indicates that they are not simply interested in making a quick sale, but that they truly care about ensuring their fox goes to a good home.

- Many reputable breeders will ensure that the fennec fox gets its required vaccines, along with a health certificate. You should discuss this with your breeder to ensure that your fox gets the required vaccines before it is released to you. You should also inquire as to whether or not this will be included in the full price.

- Because it is often difficult to find a local fennec fox breeder, you may need to have your small fox shipped to you through an airline. Does your breeder ship? How much will the shipping cost? How soon will the fox arrive? Will you need a permit if it is shipped out of state? These are all questions you should ask. Also, it's a good idea to pay extra for shipping insurance.

- Note: If you can obtain your fennec fox from a local breeder that would be the absolute best option. Not only would you get to see your fennec fox beforehand, but it is also much less of a stressful situation for your fox (assuming you don't have to travel too far).

- Your fennec fox should be hand raised from an early age and socialized in order to make it as friendly as possible, and to lessen aggressive behavior. You should ask your breeder how the fennec was raised to ensure that it was pulled from its mother by at least two weeks of age, and also socialized with humans as much as possible. A kit raised by its mother is not recommended as a pet.

- You should inquire about your fennec fox's parents. If its parents are related then your fennec will be more likely to have health issues. Cross breeding should not occur.

- In order to make your pet as comfortable as possible, it is a good idea to feed your pet the same dry food that it received when being cared for by the breeder. So, you should ask your breeder what dry foods the fennec fox received in their care. Many breeders will include a nice sample of the food with the shipment. That way you can slowly wean them from it and start feeding it another brand if necessary.

- If you're having your fennec fox shipped to you, it's a good idea to ask for pictures of the fox that you plan to purchase. This also helps to reduce the risk of purchasing from a scam artist, though it still doesn't guarantee that they're legit.

- Understand that you will very likely be placed on a waiting list (usually for a year). Hand raising fennec foxes is far from easy and there are only so many kits available every year.

- Be very suspicious of any breeder who only accepts Western Union, check, or money order. A legitimate breeder should be willing to accept Paypal as a payment.

- <u>Do your research</u>. Fennec foxes are a much desired pet, and many scam artists are aware of this. Ask your breeder for references. Use the links listed in chapter 10 to connect with other fox owners. Ask if they are familiar with your breeder, or better yet if they can recommend one.

The cost of buying a fennec from reliable breeders can be expensive due to the fact that there are  only so many kits available at any particular time, and that breeding kits can be a very daunting task. Nonetheless, don't attempt to cut corners. Do your research, and always purchase your fox from a USDA certified breeder.

C. Locating a Breeder

Thanks to internet technology, if you reside in the USA, finding a fennec fox breeder isn't very challenging (although finding a breeder that is local can be difficult).

Chapter 6. Purchasing Fennec Foxes

There are many fennec fox breeders who currently advertise their services online.

However, it appears to be much more difficult for potential fennec fox owners in the UK to locate fennec fox breeders.

For many reasons, I do not personally endorse any particular breeders. However, below you will find a few links that may help you in your search for a fennec fox breeder. Do not assume that any of these breeders are exempt from being looked into. Remember, it is your responsibility, as the potential fennec fox owner, to research the breeder and to ask the necessary questions before purchasing the fennec fox.

USA:

- FennecFoxes.net – This is by far one of the most comprehensive lists of breeders—but mostly within the USA. (If you are reading this book as a hardcopy rather than an eBook version, then go online to www.fennecfoxes.net, and click on "breeder directory" located on the upper left side to view the list).

- Creatures Great N Small – A seller of fennecs, this site owner is located in Indiana and it appears that she ships as well. (If unable to access the link, type www.CreaturesGreatNSmall.com in your web browser).

- Again, if you live in the USA you can simply Google "fennec fox breeders" and you will come across many other fennec fox breeders as well.

UK:

➢ Flashman Foxes –The owner of this site is quite knowledgeable about fennecs, and also an active moderator on Sybil's fennec forum. (Simply Google "Flashman Foxes" if unable to access link).

- Note: It is best to contact a breeder once you have at least read this book in entirety and utilized a forum if you have any further questions about fennecs. Please do not waste a breeder's time if you are not serious about owning a fennec fox.

Chapter 7. Caring For your Fennec Fox Pet

Many people want to own a fennec fox as a pet because they're cute and they think that it's a cool idea. But are you *ready* for a fennec fox? Taking care of a fennec requires dedication, know-how, patience, money, and time. Here are some of the questions that you should ask yourself to determine if you are ready to take care of a pet fennec fox.

- Are fennec foxes legal in your area and have you met all of the legal requirements?

Chapter 7. Caring For your Fennec Fox Pet

- Do you have enough time to play, entertain, supervise, and bond with your pet?

- Do you have enough energy for a fennec fox? You may have to chase your pet to get it in its cage or to retrieve an item it has, and they are fast.

- Do you have enough money to provide the needs as well as other requirements of raising a fennec fox?

- Are you ok with your fennec having accidents everywhere, and are you responsible enough to clean up after your pet?

- Can you put up with their temperament and sometimes unpredictable behavior?

- Do you have enough space in your home for a fennec fox? Foxes need space to run and play, and an apartment will not be sufficient.

- Are you or another responsible adult home most of the day? Fennec foxes should not be in their enclosures for long periods of time and should have much time to roam and play.

- Do you understand that fennecs love to dig and will often try to dig at your floors, furniture, and walls?

- Can you handle the loud noises that they make (even at night)?

Chapter 7. Caring For your Fennec Fox Pet

- Do you or are you planning on having a very young child soon? Fennecs are not recommended for children under the age of six, because they typically don't understand the proper way to handle a fox. Not to mention, you wouldn't have very much time to care for your fox if you have a very young child. Are you planning on expanding your family anytime soon?

- Are you planning on moving in the future? Fennecs aren't legal in every state and you may need to get a permit simply to transport it through certain states.

- Will there be someone other than yourself who can care for your fox in case of an emergency, or if you need to be away for a longer period of time (long work hours, etc.)?

- Can you accept that fennec foxes are normally not cuddly creatures and will usually rather be playing than in your arms?

- You can never learn too much. Are you willing to continue to educate yourself about your pet?

If you answered all of the questions appropriately, then you may be ready to own a fennec fox. Unlike domesticated pets like dogs and cats, fennec foxes have their own specific needs and it is crucial for pet owners to know what they are

Chapter 7. Caring For your Fennec Fox Pet

in order for your fennec fox to live long, healthy, and happily under your care.

A. Care of Pet Fennec Foxes

Caring for your fennec fox involves providing nutrition, training, hygiene, and a safe environment. Below are some guidelines on how to properly care for your fennec fox.

a. Bathing

In the wild, fennec foxes bathe themselves by licking themselves with their own saliva. This habit is similarly observed in cats.

For that reason, fennec foxes do not require a bath regularly. They only require bathing if they get into a mess. However, in the beginning stages it is a good idea to bathe your pet on a more regular basis, simply to train it and get it accustomed to being bathed.

It should also be noted that fennecs are afraid of running water, so prepare the bath before fetching your fennec fox. If you need to bathe your fox you can do so in the sink or the tub. Bathing your fennec fox is also a great way to eliminate flea infestation. When bathing your fox, you can use a recommended pet shampoo by your veterinarian or a mild cat shampoo will do. Choose a shampoo that has anti-flea properties to eliminate unwanted fleas. Use lukewarm water when bathing your fennec fox to ensure it is comfortable. Be advised: they don't enjoy bathing time.

B. How and What to Feed

Another important role that you have to fulfill as a pet owner is to provide nourishment to your pet fennec fox. Fennec foxes are omnivores in the wild which means that they eat both plant and animal materials.

A common pet fennec fox is usually fed canned cat and dog food by their pet owners. However, to supplement their diet, they need to have other foods as well. Fennec foxes also require a high taurine diet, thus giving them taurine pills to supplement their diet is very important.

Fennec foxes are desert animals so their bodies can conserve water for a very long time. Although they do not drink a lot of water, you still want to make sure that you put a bowl of water near in case they need it.

To be more specific, review a typical diet for a fennec fox, found on the next page:

Chapter 7. Caring For your Fennec Fox Pet

Everyday Diet

- High quality canned (wet) cat food – given as a base once or twice a day

- High quality dry dog food – often left out throughout the day for them to enjoy

- **Several** <u>insects per day</u> including crickets and mealworms

- A couple teaspoons of frozen mixed vegetables (thawed and chopped, usually mixed in with the wet cat food. Do not use canned vegetables.)

- Taurine (see next section for more info about taurine)

Snacks/Treats

- Cooked chicken (occasionally rotated in with the wet cat food, though not required)

- Cooked eggs (boiled without the shell or scrambled)

- Pinkie mice

- A bit of fresh fruit like apple slices, bananas, blueberries, strawberries, and melon (This is only a treat; too much fruit is not healthy and can cause loose stools. Do not forget to remove the seeds!)

- Dry cereal, dog treats, and dates and figs

You do not need to feed your fennec multiple snacks every day. This is simply a list of snacks that you can choose from. Be careful not to over feed your fennec.

As far as commercial dog and cat foods are concerned, you want to choose premium, high quality grain-free food that is a good source of taurine and also a great source of meat (meat should be listed as the first ingredient). Also, dog food in particular should be suitable for small breeds or puppies.

Some great options for premium dry dog foods are Royal Canin Chihuahua Puppy 30 (highly recommended), Wellness Core, Science Diet for small canines, and Taste of the Wild Brands. Some great options for canned cat food include Fancy Feast (grilled chicken or turkey), 9 Lives Veal and Gravy, or Friskies Prime Fillets (tuna or turkey).

Once again, please be advised that you cannot feed your fox just dog and/or cat food alone. That is not healthy.

If you have other pets, be sure to keep your fennec fox away from their food to ensure that your fennec is not eating any food other than its own. Also note that fennec foxes do not like being bothered when they are eating, so give them their space and allow them to enjoy their meal peacefully.

Chapter 7. Caring For your Fennec Fox Pet

Many fox owners swear by a raw food diet for their pets, as it most closely mimics what a fox would have in the wild and provides a great source of taurine, amongst other potential benefits. However feeding a fennec fox raw food is a controversial topic and many vets would not recommend it. If you are interested in a raw food diet for your pet, please research thoroughly before doing so and ask your vet about the advantages and disadvantages of that decision.

a. How Much Taurine in Fennec Diet

Fennec foxes absolutely must have taurine in their diet to remain healthy. How much taurine you need to feed your fennec fox depends on what you are feeding it on a daily basis. If you were to go with a raw food diet then you would probably *not* need to feed your fox as many taurine supplements as you would if your fox was on a commercial diet, since many raw foods are a great source of taurine.

With that being said however, it is also very difficult to overdose on taurine, as what is not needed is simply excreted. Therefore I wouldn't be concerned about providing too much. PetAg Taurine Tablets are a great choice and can be purchased online through Amazon. You should feed your fennec a minimum of one tablet per day (250 mg); but two tablets per day is highly preferred, especially if the tablets are the fennec's main source of taurine. It is possible that your fennec will take the tablet as is, but if not then you will need to crush it up a bit and mix it in with its food. Another option is taurine powder which you can measure and sprinkle on your pet's food. NOW Foods Taurine Pure Powder is a good option which can also be purchased on Amazon. Taurine is an essential part of a fennec's diet and if not provided, your fox will likely develop many serious health issues.

C. Foods to Avoid

As a general rule, what is not good for your pet cat or dog is also not good for your fennec fox.

It is important for pet owners to be careful with the kinds of food that they feed their fennec foxes. An unhealthy diet can be fatal to your pet.

Fennec foxes should not be fed anything with cooked or fragile bones because they can easily break and lacerate their throats. Pet owners should also avoid feeding their fennec foxes spicy foods. Moreover, feeding them foods high in acidic content can also cause ulcers in their stomachs.

Fennec foxes are naturally curious animals thus they may wolf down anything that they can get to, such as shopping bags, small toys, and any small objects that they may find around the home. Therefore it is important to be tidy and eliminate access to all of these types of things that can make them sick or cause them to choke. Furthermore, you should

Chapter 7. Caring For your Fennec Fox Pet

not allow your pet fennec to eat table food. They will prefer table food over their own and this will become a problem.

Here is a more exhaustive list of actual foods that are toxic to fennec foxes:

- Any Chocolate, Cocoa Beans, or Hulls – extremely fatal, especially for a small 3 lb. fennec fox.

- Raw Salmon – highly toxic; contains a parasite with a mortality rate of about 90%.

- Coffee, Tea, and other Caffeine – can cause vomiting, coma, tremors, diarrhea, seizures, and even death.

- Grapes and Raisins – can cause hyperkalemia, kidney damage, and vomiting.

- Macadamia Nuts and Walnuts – can cause weakness, vomiting, and tremors although poisoning is not common.

- Onions, Onion Powder, Garlic, and Chives – contains disulfides when ingested in huge quantities and can cause damage to red blood cells or stomach irritation.

- Tomatoes, Peppers, and Eggplant – contains glycoalkaloids which is toxic to fennecs (though tomatoes are usually fine when ripened).

- Green Potatoes, Potato Peelings, and Rhubarb Leaves – contain toxic chemicals to fennecs like chaconine, solanine, calcium oxalates, and glycoalkaloids.

- Xylitol (artificial sweetener) – this is a compound found in toothpastes, baked goods, candy, and chewing gum and is toxic to fennecs which can lead to liver damage or worse, failure.

- Fruit Pits & Seeds – pits from apples, cherries, peaches, pears, etc. are found to hold small amounts of the toxic substance cyanide. While a few may not cause harm, it will become a problem if consumed regularly overtime.

- Avocadoes – can cause diarrhea, vomiting, and difficulties breathing.

- Wild Mushrooms – can contain very dangerous toxins which could cause liver damage and/or death.

- Nutmeg – this spice can cause seizures as well as death.

- Corn on the Cob – can cause allergies and also lead to intestinal obstruction which could be fatal.

- Salt and Sugar – too much salt can cause kidney failure, and of course too much sugar can cause obesity amongst other things.

- Dairy – dairy products are usually high in fat and can cause diarrhea and gas.

- Beef, Pork, Ham, and Turkey Skin – fatty foods, especially fatty meats can cause vomiting, diarrhea, loss of appetite, and pain. Fennec foxes need meat in their diet, but avoid fatty meats. Also turkey itself is perfectly fine, but it is the skin that should be avoided.

- Yeast (alone or in dough form) – causes gas and discomfort, and can rupture the stomach.

- Feeding your fennec fox foods high in fiber is not recommended (for example grains, and *too many* fruits and veggies).

- Alcohol – I think this goes without saying, but if your fennec fox gets to alcohol this could cause vomiting, diarrhea, and death.

- Pennies – although not a food, it should be noted that pennies can cause kidney failure and be incredibly lethal, as they contain a high amount of zinc. Even one penny could cause severe damage or death, especially if not removed.

- Note: A *few* of these items *may* be ok if fed in moderation, but it's better to be safe than sorry. You have a responsibility to your fennec fox. Please keep these foods and items out of its reach. Always read food labels. If you suspect that your fennec fox has eaten any of these items, call your veterinarian immediately. If you can't reach your veterinarian, call your local animal emergency clinic or the Animal Poison Control Center (ASPCA) at 888-426-4435. There may be charges associated with calling ASPCA.

D. Training a Fennec Fox

Training is another important task that you need to partake in with your fennec fox. When training fennec foxes, it is important to take note that there is a big difference between training dogs and fennec foxes.

Although both animals are similar in some ways, they are hardly the same such that dogs are easier to train while fennec foxes are much more challenging. This does not mean that fennec foxes are not intelligent creatures. Like all foxes, they are actually very intelligent. However, their playful behavior as well as their curiosity makes them very difficult to train.

Moreover, their inability to respond to praises makes them very difficult to train. The succeeding subheadings will discuss more about the different trainings that your fennec fox can undergo.

Chapter 7. Caring For your Fennec Fox Pet

a. Can You Train Them?

As mentioned earlier, it is possible to train fennec foxes provided that you dedicate more time while training them. Training fennec foxes is integral in building a bond between you and your pet fennec fox.

The secret to training fennec foxes is to begin training them very young until they reach adulthood. Moreover, it is also important to constantly train fennec foxes so that they do not revert back to their natural habits and instincts.

Fennec foxes can be trained to behave while bathing, while being handled, and while being put on a harness, amongst other things. They can also be trained to do limited tricks such as fetching a particular item or sitting, but again this takes work and time.

When training fennec foxes, praising them is not as effective compared to giving them treats like a dog snack for example. Unlike dogs, fennec foxes don't have a great desire to please their owners, thus they perform well under a reward based system where they actually receive something tangible in return, such as a treat every time they complete a particular task, rather than just giving them praise.

Another thing that you need to take note of while training fennec foxes is that they have the habit of nipping. Fennec foxes communicate in the wild by taking small bites that do not break the skin and if it is your first time handling them, you might be surprised or even shocked with such behavior.

To curb their biting habit, do not play with your pets with your hands or with your fingers. Do not reward their biting activities. Never "play bite" with your fox as that would cause the fox to think that biting is ok, which would send it mix signals. Use a toy to play bite with your fox instead, but never tolerate it biting you. If they do bite, tell them "No" or instead place a toy in their mouths. If they respond by biting the toy instead of your fingers, give them a reward.

When you are initiating play time, you should get on the floor with your fox. They are far more likely to come to you and play with you when you are seated and more on their level. If you are standing they will want to play chase. Furthermore, they often associate you chasing them with you wanting to put them back into their cage, which they obviously don't like. For that reason you should also begin to play with your fox once you are standing with it in your arms. That way it won't associate you picking it up with the end of play time (it likely will not want to be held for too long, but that's fine).

Training fennec foxes requires repetitive actions and it may take you weeks or even months to fully train them to do things that you want. Patience is imperative.

On the other hand, it is important to never punish or hurt your fennec fox. Just like children, the best way to train pets is to use positive reinforcement. If you punish your pet by hitting or spanking it, you will make it more fearful and you can potentially damage the bond between you and your pet severely. Moreover, your fennec fox may have a problem associating the punishment and what it did wrong. Not to mention, fennecs are very fragile and you could cause physical harm, which is just unacceptable. For this reason, positive reinforcement is the best way to train them.

b. Clicker Training

Clicker training is basically a training technique which uses positive reinforcement. It is the process of training your pet to respond to a distinct sound (a click) which indicates a desired behavioral outcome from your pet that is followed by a reward for doing the desired behavior. For example, if your fennec uses the bathroom in its litter box, you would hit the clicker to get its attention and immediately feed it a treat. Using this technique, your fox will associate the good behavior with the clicker sound and a tasty treat.

Since fennec foxes respond better with positive reinforcement training, this is a great technique to try. For a clicker and more information on clicker training and the proper steps, please click here or Google "clicker training". You may also be interested in purchasing Peggy Tillman's "Clicking with Your Dog"", a step by step guide on clicker training including pictures (which of course, you can purchase on Amazon).

c. Litter Training

One of the things that make fennec foxes so great is that unlike other exotic pets, they do not exude strong body odor.

However, fennec foxes are considered the most difficult of all types of wild canines to litter train. It is nearly impossible to completely litter train fennec foxes. Fennec foxes typically just "go" whenever they need to, often not even stopping what they're doing. Even if you are somewhat successful with litter training, they will still have accidents and will likely never be 100% litter trained. If a fennec fox owner decides to take on this difficult task, then it is their responsibility to litter train the fennec fox once purchased. When you buy your fennec fox from a breeder, do not assume that your pet will already be litter trained.

Although litter training fennec foxes is difficult, I have included some info on doing so, in case you are interested.

It is said that most fennec foxes mimic the behaviors of other animals or pets around them thus if you have a litter trained cat, your fennec fox can learn from the behavior of your cat. Although this can help, it is still important that you actively participate in potty training your pet fennec fox as well.

When potty training, you can either use litter boxes or puppy pads. However, if you decide to use a litter box, make sure that you do not purchase clay litter. Use a non-clumping litter made from paper pellets or other materials so that they do not stick to the bottom of your fox's paws.

The paws of fennec foxes are laden with fur and clay pellets tend to adhere on the fur over time. This often causes pain to your fennec foxes especially if the clay has dried up. Moreover, clay pellets tend to form dust and accumulate just about everywhere.

Fennec foxes are good diggers in the wild thus it is important to buy covered litter boxes to discourage the fennec foxes from playing with the litter. If your fox is going to have access to more than one room in your house, you should consider placing a litter box in each room to prevent your fennec fox from relieving itself anywhere.

On the other hand, some fennecs want to relieve themselves in their cages, thus you should make sure that their cages are accessible and put a litter box inside the cage as well. Putting litter boxes in virtually every room in the house is the best way to make your fennec fox used to relieving itself in appropriate places. However, it is important that you introduce one designated litter area overtime to completely potty train your fennec fox. This also helps you save a lot of time when it comes to cleaning up after your pet.

Potty training your fennec fox can be challenging, but you have to be patient. It is important that you start training it while it is still young. Be sure to bring your fennec fox to the litter box after feeding it. Whether or not they relieve themselves after feeding, you still need to take them near the litter box so that they develop this particular habit after every feeding.

Whenever your fennec fox has accidents in the house and relieves itself in random places, do not punish it. Take it to the litter box instead, even if it has already relieved itself previously. As part of positive reinforcement, give them treats every time they successfully use the litter box and/or use clicker training if you have decided to incorporate that technique.

Litter training your fennec fox will be challenging and it is important that you have enough patience and determination to see it through its training. Let me reiterate that although these are all great tips for litter training a fennec, it is still *very* difficult to do so. So, if the inability to litter train your fennec is a deal-breaker for you, then this pet isn't a good choice.

Lastly, always clean up after your fennec fox. Fennec foxes may not emit strong body odors but not cleaning up after their stool and/or urine immediately is unhygienic. Not to mention, fennec foxes mark their territory often, and if you don't clean up after them you will encourage them to mark even more.

Be sure to also keep the litter boxes clean. Litter boxes should be cleaned daily.

d. Harness and Leash Training

Fennec foxes are highly agile animals, thus even with a harness and leash they can still slip away from you. This is especially true if they're in an area where they don't feel safe, or if there is too much commotion or loudness. They can become very startled and skittish. The problem with a runaway fennec fox is you will have great trouble getting it back. For this reason, if you need to take your fennec outside (to the vet for example), I highly recommend that you use a cat-sized travel crate or per carrier.

E. Ideal Environment

In their natural environment, fennec foxes are capable of digging holes that are twenty feet deep. Moreover, their ability to dig holes into the ground also allows them to create furrows where they live, breed, and take care of their young. This is the reason why fennec foxes in captivity tend to dig holes in the garden or prefer hiding under the furniture if they have the chance.

For this reason, the best environment for fennec foxes in captivity is to be kept indoors. If they are outside without a proper enclosure, it would be very easy for them to dig their way out and run away. However, when indoors they should not be in their cage unless you're sleeping at night and/or away for short periods of time. Fennec foxes are very hyper, and vivacious animals and they need to be able to play, run around, and release their energy. A fennec fox kept in a cage for long periods of time will be very unhappy and will become disobedient and aggressive. It may even self-mutilate.

Fennec foxes are most comfortable in a climate of 75-90 degrees Fahrenheit (24° -32°C), which is another reason why it is recommended that they are mainly, if not always, kept indoors (especially during the winter).

a. Indoor Enclosures

You can keep your fennec fox inside your home at all times. In fact, for several reasons, it is highly recommended. However, when keeping your fennec inside, you have to take into consideration your living situation.

Fennec foxes can be noisy, even during nighttime, thus if you live in an apartment the noise will definitely rouse up your neighbors. For this reason, keeping fennec foxes in apartment flats is not advisable.

When keeping your fennec inside of your home, make sure that you keep it inside an enclosure if you are not around to oversee. A fennec fox unsupervised will likely cause damage to belongings and/or itself and consume anything within its reach.

Every fennec fox should have an inside enclosure. Even if you plan on building an outdoor enclosure to use

Chapter 7. Caring For your Fennec Fox Pet

sporadically, you will need to bring your fennec fox inside and you will *not* be able to supervise it at all times. Thus an inside enclosure is necessary. A large dog crate is sufficient, but a large Ferret Nation cage is highly recommended as it is well constructed and designed with sufficient space. Normally you can find a Ferret Nation cage priced between $200-$250 on eBay. I would recommend the 2-level, Ferret Nation model 142 and also purchase a third level add on if possible. You should also purchase ferret ramp covers to place over the ramps in order to protect your fennec's paws. You can find ferret ramp covers on eBay as well. Please double check with your state and county on cage requirements as some areas have specific guidelines.

Inside of your fennec's cage, you should have their food, water, and litter pan if applicable. Don't forget about your fennec's bed as well. A ferret bed or hammock will suffice. It's a good idea to purchase more than one because your fennec will likely urinate in its bed while sleeping. Therefore you should always have a clean bed available while you wash and sanitize the other. Many fennecs love blankets as well so you may want to lay a blanket down in its cage also. Your fennecs' cage should be cleaned every day and you should place fresh food and water in the cage daily as well.

When you are supervising your fennec fox, leave the cage door open throughout the day so that it is accessible to your fennec and your fox is able to return to its cage at any time. Your fennec may want to nap throughout the day here and there, and it may feel more comfortable doing so in its cage.

Furthermore, this helps the fennec to view the cage less as a restriction, and more as a home. Only leave the cage open however, when you are overseeing your fennec. If you are sleeping, not in the home, or simply not supervising your fennec at that point and time, put it in its cage and keep the cage door closed and locked.

To stimulate their natural behaviors, you should also purchase a sandbox so your fennec has something to dig in. This will help to prevent your fox from digging elsewhere (not completely, but it will be a big help). Designating a particular space where your fennec fox can scratch and dig to its heart's content is one of the best things you can do.
To introduce your fox to the sandbox, it helps if you pretend to dig in the sandbox as well. You can purchase a sandbox on Amazon or eBay in the $30-$70 price range. You may also be able to purchase a sandbox at a local store in your area, depending on the time of year.

Some owners even provide their fennec fox with its own room for their enjoyment which they "fox proof". If you are interested in doing so, please be sure to add many toys and things for their enrichment. Cat towers, play toys, cat teasers, things to climb on, hiding places, shelves, and of course sandboxes, all provide great fun and enjoyment for fennec foxes. Of course, do not forget to also fox proof the room, but more about that later.

Once more, it is important to take note that you should not place your fennec fox in its enclosure frequently, or for long periods of time. A fox that is constantly in its cage will not be a happy fox and it will show it. When you are around the house and able to supervise, take your fennec out so that it can explore its environment. This is also a good way for your pet fennec fox to bond with you – the pet owner.

When you first take your fennec out of its cage, allow it to run around and release its energy. Once it has done so for a while, *then* that's a good time to attempt to play and bond with your fennec fox. But understand that it needs time to run free.

b. Outdoor Enclosures

Although it is not necessary, some owners do provide their fennecs with outside enclosures. Unlike indoor enclosures, outdoor enclosures for fennec foxes usually require much more money, preparation, and thought. You will need to do much planning ahead if building an outdoor enclosure.

For starters, it is recommended that the outside enclosure has a minimum dimension of 10ft x 10ft to encourage your pet to run around and get some exercise. The outdoor enclosure should be made from high quality chain links which are used to create cyclone fences. You would also need to add chicken wire on the outside of the chain link to prevent the fennec's head from getting trapped in the chain links.

If your fennec is just a kit however, you should not have it in an outside enclosure. Not only is this potentially

Chapter 7. Caring For your Fennec Fox Pet

dangerous for your fennec, but it should be inside the home, bonding with you at that age.

Fennec foxes are also good climbers, thus it is important that their outdoor enclosures have fencing at the top. Moreover, reinforcing the bottom of their outside enclosure is absolutely necessary to prevent the fennec fox from digging its way out. You will therefore need to add fencing at the bottom of the enclosure as well. Once done, cover the floor with soil, sand, straw or wooden chips as this mimics their natural environment and it stimulates their playfulness as well as their curiosity. Don't forget to add their food, water, and litter box.

You should also add secondary fencing, (if you do not have it). This will help to ensure that the public and also other animals stay away from your pet fennec whilst it is in your backyard.

c. Proofing Your Home

While it is important to keep your fennec fox inside its enclosure if you are not around to supervise it, it is also crucial to let your fennec out of its cage when inside your home, so that it can explore its surroundings. Before doing this however, it is important to fox proof the area your fennec fox will have access to.

Chapter 7. Caring For your Fennec Fox Pet

You must understand that fennec foxes get into much more mischief when they are bored. So in order to lessen destructive behavior you have to keep them preoccupied. You should provide your fennec with toys and also make playtime with your fennec a regular occasion as well. Otherwise you can expect a damaging little creature.

Fennec foxes are small and agile animals, thus proofing your home can be quite a task. Aside from being small, fennec foxes also love climbing and digging onto the ground. Having a carpet and a fennec around would spell disaster for your carpet with its digging and marking activities. The best suggestion here is to remove carpets. You could also provide you fennec with cheap rugs or mats to dig on, but those would have to be regularly cleaned as well.

To make your home fennec fox-proof, make sure that you remove anything that they can easily get to that they should not have. You should relocate any house plants that are accessible to them and avoid putting out food (or other objects) not suitable for them within their reach. Moreover, always close the doors to rooms that you do not want your fennec fox to enter.

Fennecs can mark on anything including lamps, furniture, tables, and more. You should therefore use covers on your furniture (unless it's leather which is easy to clean). Also you need to clean up their markings right away and erase their smell so that they don't come back and mark the spot over and over again.

Fennecs love rubber and shiny and metallic items. They will steal anything they find intriguing in a blink of an eye if you're not careful. So try to remove shiny and rubbery things that are easily accessible, and watch your fox carefully or else it may eat items which could be disastrous for its health. On the other hand, a great method of curbing this particular behavior of chewing up on things is to give them toys that are practically *theirs* to chew on (as long as the fennec can't actually chew the toy into pieces and swallow any parts of it).

Aside from shiny and rubbery things, be careful with any small objects left lying around the house. Keep your floors clean at all times. Even wires and rope like objects should be kept off the ground as your pet fennec can get entangled in them or chew on them.

You need to cover your electrical sockets as well. Also ensure that your fennec cannot get to any dangerous substances like bleach or other chemicals.

Do not place easily breakable objects on low lying areas or areas which the fennec can easily reach with a jump. Remember, fennecs can jump pretty high for their size, so don't leave your food or drinks alone on the table. Be especially careful not to leave out any drugs or medication. The fennec is a very small animal and one swallowed pill could potentially do a lot of damage.

Chapter 7. Caring For your Fennec Fox Pet

Don't forget to close your toilet seat and keep your bathroom door closed. Remember to keep all windows and doors closed that you don't want your pet to access. Window screens should be in good condition in order to keep your pet fennec inside the house. As once they get loose, you have a very slim chance of ever finding them.

Before purchasing a fennec fox, it is crucial to make their homes fox-proof in order to prevent any unfortunate accidents from happening within the home.

F. Medical Problems of Fennec Foxes

Fennec foxes can live up to 16 years in captivity and are generally healthy animals. They are susceptible to diseases that also affect both cats and dogs however. It is important for pet owners to take their fennec fox to a veterinarian for annual checkups as well as the administration of certain vaccines.

Below are some common medical problems/diseases of fennec foxes that pet owners should be wary of. The list is exhaustive simply for informative purposes, so don't be alarmed. If you care for your fox properly and ensure the proper vaccines are administered by your vet then your fox will likely be a very healthy fox.

Understand that I am not a doctor and the purpose of this section is to simply inform you of some of the diseases that can occur in a fennec fox. You should not use this information in an attempt to diagnose or treat your pet. If you are under the impression that your fennec fox is not well then it is your responsibility to contact your veterinarian for instructions and treatment.

- Intestinal parasite infestation – like dogs, fennec foxes are prone to worm infestations which include tape worms and round worms. Pet fennec foxes that are heavily infested with worms experience rapid weight loss. For this reason, it is important for pet owners to de-worm fennec foxes regularly.

- Fleas – another health problem a fennec foxes may experience is flea infestation. Fleas from other animals like stray cats or dogs can easily be transmitted to fennec foxes.

- Canine Distemper – a viral disease that affects animals such as ferrets, cats, and dogs. The disease agent is a single-stranded RNA virus from the paramyxovirus family. This particular disease can be threatening or not depending on the immune system of the fennec foxes. However, it is one of the main reasons for mortality in young pups. Fennec foxes get infected with the virus through contact with animals that are already infected. The signs and symptoms include nose discharges, gooey eyes, fever, poor appetite and the presence of cough. Fortunately, there are now vaccines that can be used to treat fennec foxes that are infected with canine distemper.

- Trauma (bite wounds) – fennecs can easily get into a commotion with other dogs and can also get bitten by them. These are some of the common clinical syndromes that fennecs get into.

- Neonatal death – this refers to fennec kits that die due to 'nervous mothering'.

- Neoplasia – formation and growth of tissues where it is not needed which can become cancerous. The cause is unknown.

- Renal Disease – this is the destruction of the fennecs' kidneys. It can be caused by many factors but mainly due to food intake.

- Liver Disease – this is the destruction of the liver organ of the fennec could be due to high doses of medicine, food intake or a hereditary factor—causes are really not known but these could be risk factors.

- Cardiomyopathy – this is the death of heart tissues. The cause is unknown.

- Pneumonia – this is an inflamed lung caused by an infection by a bacteria or a virus.

- Dermatitis – is an inflammation of the skin caused by mites.

- Conjunctivitis – is the inflammation of the conjunctiva of the eye which is caused by a virus or bacteria.

- Corneal lesions – this is tearing of the cornea due to a foreign object or trauma to the eye.

- Glaucoma – this is an irreversible, gradual and permanent loss of vision especially if left untreated. This is caused by an increasing eye pressure.

- Histoplasmosis – this disease affects the lungs of the fennec and is fatal if not treated. This is caused by inhalation of a fungus that thrives in excretions like feces, vomit, and urine.

- Taurine deficiency – taurine deficiency can cause many health issues with your fennec, including decreased vision or blindness, and/or heart failure.

*Again, this list is exhaustive for informational purposes, so do not be alarmed. Most of these diseases affect a dog or a cat just as easily. As long as you care for your fennec properly, it is unlikely to become seriously ill.

Chapter 8. Things You Should Know About Fennec Foxes

Fennec foxes have unique traits. They are playful just like dogs, but they are sometimes aloof just like cats. With the unique temperament of fennec foxes, it is very important for pet owners to know about the characteristics of fennec foxes before purchasing one.

A. Are They Noisy Pets?

One of the most common questions pet owners ask is whether fennec foxes are noisy pets. Some fennecs are not as noisy as others but for the most part they are noisy pets, many of them even at nighttime. In the wild, fennec foxes

Chapter 8. Things You Should Know About Fennec Foxes

are naturally nocturnal which means that they are active at nighttime. This behavior is an adaptation so that they can conserve their energy amidst the harsh and hot desert environment. It is *possible* that if you interact and play with your fennec a lot during the day, that overtime the fennec will adapt to your schedule. But that would take time.

Fennec foxes make different kinds of sounds. They sometime make a bird-like call during nighttime. This call is their way of communicating with other fennec foxes in the wild. They bark or snarl when they are involved in fierce play or if they are showing their aggression, or even if they're bored at night. When they are lonely, they tend to wail piteously or they can squeal with delight when their pet owners play with them. What makes them very unique from dogs is that they have the ability to purr especially when they are satisfied and happy.

Barking fennec foxes at night can definitely be disturbing, but it may help if you play with your fennec before bedtime. Also, it is a good idea to place your fennec's cage in a room further away from yours to help eliminate the noise.

B. Spaying/Neutering

Male fennec foxes can be aggressive especially when they reach sexual maturity. They also tend to show their aggression if they interact with other male fennec foxes. For this reason, most pet owners opt for their male fennec foxes to be neutered. Neutering fennec foxes involve the removal of the reproductive organ of your pet. Spaying is a term used on female animals.

a. Advantages Of Spaying Or Neutering

There are a lot of advantages of spaying or neutering fennec foxes. Listed below are the reasons why pet owners should consider sterilizing their fennec foxes.

- Male aggression can be minimized. Neutering reduces the male hormone levels which are concentrated in the male reproductive organ. In fact, neutered males are often found to be more affectionate than those that are not neutered.

- Neutered or spayed fennec foxes also have reduced strength of body smell thus they are more hygienic than those that haven't undergone the procedure.

- Spaying female foxes also prevents unwanted pregnancy. However, pet owners who plan to breed their fennec foxes should not consider this procedure so that they can give birth to litters of fennec foxes in the future.

Chapter 8. Things You Should Know About Fennec Foxes

b. Disadvantages of Spaying or Neutering

There are also disadvantages to spaying or neutering fennec foxes that pet owners should know before they decide to let their pets undergo such procedure.

- Fennec foxes have a low tolerance to anesthetics and an overdose can often kill a fennec fox. For this reason, you need to make sure your vet is experienced with giving anesthesia to very small animals.

- Spayed or neutered fennec foxes are at risk of becoming obese. The decrease in their hormone levels also increases their food intake. You will have to monitor their diet closely.

- They may require intensive care while recovering after the procedure unlike other animals.

Deciding whether you should neuter or spay your fennec foxes depend on your preferences. If you are not planning on breeding them, then your best option is to neuter them.

However, you have to look for a qualified veterinarian that can carry out the procedure properly to avoid risking your pet's well-being.

Chapter 8. Things You Should Know About Fennec Foxes

C. Fur Shedding

Fennec foxes have thick fur which they have developed as a form of adaptation to their environment. Their fur helps them conserve their body heat and insulate them from the cold desert nights.

Since fennec foxes have thick fur, most pet owners fear that they are prone to shedding their fur frequently. However, unlike dogs or cats, fennec foxes rarely shed their fur and if they do, they do it periodically as their response to the changing weather.

Fennec fox owners can brush the coat of their fennec foxes daily, but again, they will not shed much.

D. Smell

Fennec foxes do not require baths on a regular basis and they do not have a strong smell unlike other exotic pets. Although this may be the case, they do emit foul and musky odor from their scent glands when they are scared or surprised. The scent glands of fennec foxes are found at the tip of their tail.

Although fennec foxes do not exude foul body odor, this does not mean that their urine as well as feces do not smell. Fennec fox urine smells a lot like skunk spray. However, the odor can be neutralized if pet owners clean on a regular basis and use appropriate cleaning products. If you have carpet however, I'm afraid there is only so much that you can do to eliminate the urine odor. Carpet is not recommended if you own a fennec.

On the other hand, the smell of the urine and feces of fennec foxes is also attributed to the kind of diet that they eat. Thus it is important to feed fennec foxes a balanced diet.

E. Personality of Fennec Foxes as Pets

Fennec foxes are adorable pets but they do come with behaviors and personalities that are unique. Fennec foxes have personalities that are similar to both a cat and a dog in certain ways. They are similar to a dog in that they are high energy and playful (although a fennec is much more energetic). Yet they are similar to a cat in that they are fairly independent. Fennecs will very rarely seek you out for affection and usually are pretty aloof. Although they typically don't reject petting or physical contact from their owners, they don't necessarily seek it out either. Unlike dogs, they don't have a great desire to please their owners. They will come to you, but on their own terms. They can be very sweet at times but they usually don't like to be held for too long. They love to run around, play, and explore.

Chapter 9. Precautions to Take with your Fennec Fox

Although fennecs may not be the perfect exotic pet for every family, there are still plenty of people who are interested in caring for them. So, it is important for potential owners to know about important precautions that one must take. After all, fennec foxes are exotic animals and even if they have been socialized, there are certain things that you should do and certain things that you should *not* do to protect your fox and others.

A. At Home

Although fennecs can be fun and sweet at times, they can still turn into aggressive pets when handled inappropriately. Below is a discussion of some of the things that you need to be aware of when caring for your fennec fox at home.

a. Fennec Foxes and Children

Fennec foxes can make great family pets and they are great with children. However, it is important to supervise small children when interacting with fennec foxes. This is especially true because children are very curious and they

Chapter 9. Precautions to Take with your Fennec Fox

might end up pulling the fur or the tail of fennec fox. When threatened, a fennec fox may bite a child.

Further, fennecs are not appropriate for households with children aged six and below, even if they are supervised at all times. At that age children are just not aware of how to properly handle a fox.

For older children, you need to speak with the in regards to proper behavior involving fennecs and pets as a whole. You have to teach them how to handle a fennec properly in order to avoid future problems or mistreating the fox and consequentially causing danger. As long as the child is aware of what to do and what not to do, then they can have a wonderful and rewarding relationship with the fennec. Even so, it is not recommended to leave a child and a fennec fox alone unsupervised.

b. Fennec Foxes and Other Pets

Fennec foxes usually get along fine with other pets that are of a larger size, especially those that they have grown up with. It's likely that your fennec fox will get along better with a dog (as long as it's not a hunting species), more so than with a cat however. Cats sometimes get irritated by the fennec's hyperactivity.

Chapter 9. Precautions to Take with your Fennec Fox

It is best that you never ever leave your pets alone together unsupervised, even if they appear to be getting along well.

Take extra precaution during the early stage of introducing your fennec and another pet to ensure a smooth introduction. Take it very slow at first. It's a good idea to start off by keeping your fennec in its crate to get the other animals use to its scent first.

Pet owners who happen to own smaller pets such as rodents, rabbits, turtles, and small birds should keep their small pets way beyond the reach of their fennec fox. A fennec fox will attempt to make a meal out of an animal smaller than itself.

c. Fennec Foxes and House Guests

Some fennec foxes are friendlier than others all depending on how they were raised and if they were socialized. Still, some fennec foxes will feel uncomfortable or even afraid around strangers and may retreat to avoid them. If so, you should discourage others who might want to pet your fox, otherwise your fennec fox, like other pets, might bite out of fear. Remember fennec foxes also release their violent gland when they are fearful, so the smell may send your company running for the door (though the smell goes as fast as it comes). As far as fennecs and strangers are concerned, it is best not to allow complete strangers to touch your pet.

Chapter 9. Precautions to Take with your Fennec Fox

On the other hand, if your company is not disturbing your fox, your fennec fox may not be bothered by your company at all. Moreover, some fennec foxes love all people they meet, while others are very shy. It really depends on its personality. As you spend time with your fennec you'll get to know its personality and what to expect, but always use caution.

There are times when it's best to put your fennec fox in its cage or enclosure while you're with company for a short time. This is especially true if your company is or has a small child. Keep in mind that even when your fox is in its enclosure you want to ensure that your company is not upsetting your pet by putting their fingers in the cage or any of that sort of behavior.

d. You and Your Fennec at Home

Outside of fox proofing you home, and safety measures that you need to take when you have house guests or other pets, there are also some general precautions that you should take with your fennec.

You know by now that fennecs are very hyper animals and lightning-fast as well. Your fennec may be in one area one minute and right beside you the next. Because of this, it is possible to accidently step on your small pet. However, what you can do to help prevent this is purchase a collar

Chapter 9. Precautions to Take with your Fennec Fox

with a bell for your fennec. This way, even if you have your back turned or you don't see your fennec, you'll still know when it's around.

Another thing that you should be aware of is that some fennecs do *not* enjoy being rubbed on the belly at all. Every fennec is different, but it is a good idea to start off slow by petting your fennec between the ears and allowing it to get use to you. Then after some time, you can try rubbing its belly to see how it responds. However, you should never try to force belly rubs.

Furthermore, you should clip your fennec's nails occasionally. When they are very long and sharp they can scratch you pretty good.

B. In Public

You may be considering taking your fennec out in public. However, it should be noted that fennecs cannot be easily trusted in public places. Thus it is important to understand what could happen in that particular situation.

a. Fennec Foxes and Public Paces

If given the right opportunity, a fennec fox will run away. They do not have the same type of loyalty that you would expect from a dog, for example. For this reason if a pet owner insists on taking their fennec fox outside it is best to build a proper enclosure in their yard where the fox can run, enjoy the sun, and get exercise. Remember, fennec foxes are escape artists so you will need to be very thorough when building your outside enclosure. The specifications of the enclosures for fennec foxes can be found in Chapter 7.

Another reason it is not recommended to bring your pet fennec fox into public places is because people are bound to notice them due to how cute they are. While that may seem like a great thing, you could be asking for trouble. Adults and/or children may be really tempted to pet your fennec fox. Fennec foxes have different personalities, but most are pretty shy and only want to be picked up or petted on their own terms, especially if they are not familiar with the individual. Your fennec fox may bite a stranger. This could lead to a domino effect of negative events that can ultimately lead to the euthanasia (painless killing) of your pet by authorities. Remember, this isn't a common pet. Owning an exotic pet means different rules and regulations. Even if your fennec has received a rabies shot, authorities can still euthanize it if it bites someone, being that it is an exotic animal.

Further, other people may resent your owning of an exotic pet. Some will preach about why these animals should be left in the wild, or simply be uncomfortable with knowing that a fox is in their neighborhood. Luckily fennecs are often mistaken for Chihuahuas and they don't appear to be

Chapter 9. Precautions to Take with your Fennec Fox

threatening due to their size, so this might not be a huge issue. Nonetheless, if you insist on taking your fennec outside, the best way to give your pet some outside time is within the limits of your backyard in a secured enclosure, when the weather permits.

Taking care of a fennec fox requires much attention and it is important to take heed of these precautions in order to prevent any unfortunate accidents involving your fennec fox.

Chapter 10. Helpful Sites

Becoming an owner of an exotic animal like fennec foxes is a 24/7 job, yet it can be a highly rewarding one. It is inevitable to experience instances where you are at a loss on what to do when it comes to your fennec's behavior, or you run out of ideas on how to entertain you pet, or you get baffled with your fennec's antics.

In order to help you get through these times, I have handpicked a couple of sites that would help you through this. And in time you will become an expert on fennecs and will be of help to other fennec pet owners too.

A. Forums on Fennecs

If you have read all the available information out there and would want to compare notes with other fennec pet owners, then you should try joining a forum. There are a couple of available forums out there who cater to exotic pets and even fennec pets alone. In these forums, you get to meet pet owners like yourself, ask questions or ask for advice, and even provide your input and opinion.

Chapter 10. Helpful Sites

Note: If you are reading this in paperback form, simply google the name of these links and you will be able to find these sites without a problem.

a. Forums in the USA

Sybil's Den – this forum site indubitably has the most plentiful information about fennecs. The members and moderators are really knowledgeable and helpful which you can glean from their experienced advises. In order to join the forum you need to be a member first which is quick and easy to do by registering online. This would be a great forum to utilize in regards to locating a breeder and/or a vet, asking questions about fennecs, sharing your personal experiences, and more. Happy messaging with your new co-fennec pet owners!

Note: You can utilize this forum regardless of where you're located. Just keep in mind that most of the users appear to reside in the USA.

b. Forums in the UK

Reptile Forums UK – although this forum seems to primarily focus on reptiles, there is a section where you can inquire about fennecs. Be sure to post you questions or inquires under the "exotic mammal" section.

B. Online Fennec Sellers

Here is a quick list of online fennec sellers for you to choose from.

a. US sellers

FennecFoxes.net – This is by far one of the most comprehensive lists of breeders in the whole world—but mostly within the USA.

Creatures Great N Small – A seller of fennecs, this site owner is located in Indiana and it appears that she ships as well.

b. Sellers in Europe

Flashman Foxes –The owner of this site is quite knowledgeable about fennecs, and also an active moderator on Sybil's fennec forum.

C. Exotic Pet Veterinarian

As discussed earlier in previous chapters, your fennec fox needs to be overlooked by a veterinarian in order to be provided with the right medical needs.

You also need to call each veterinary service beforehand to ensure that the vet clinic will accept an exotic pet like the fennec fox and to ensure that they have the expertise or experience in doing so.

So here is a list to help you get started on choosing one.

a. US Exotic Pet Veterinary Services

Association of Exotic Mammal Veterinarians – This is a comprehensive site of exotic veterinarians located within the USA and a handful of other countries.

Local Vets – This is another website that offers plenty of information about veterinarians. They also have a listing of vet clinics in each State of the USA.

VetScape – This is an online site that has a wide ranging list of exotic veterinarians in practice not only within the UK and USA but also worldwide.

b. UK Exotic Pet Veterinary Services

VetScape – This is an online site that has a wide ranging list of exotic veterinarians in practice not only within the UK and USA but also worldwide.

Manor Vets – Offers veterinary services to exotic pets 24/7. They have four locations in UK namely Halesowen, Edgbaston, Northfield and Cradley Heath.

D. Other

If you have the opportunity to go to a local breeder or zoo that houses fennec foxes, that is one of the best things that you can do before you decide whether or not you want to purchase a fennec. However, due to there not being many nearby breeders or zoos that house fennecs, most people don't have that luxury.

Nonetheless, there are several videos of fennec foxes online where you can see them in action. You can see how they interact with other people, how they interact with other pets, their everyday behavior, and even hear for yourself the many noises that they make.

Chapter 10. Helpful Sites

YouTube.com – This is a great site to visit to see fennec foxes on the move. Just do a search for "fennec fox" and take a look at the many videos available.

Here are a few hand-picked YouTube videos that you should take a moment to review:

- Fennec making loud noises – This is a good video to give you an idea of just how loud fennecs can be when they are excited.

If unable to access the above link, go to youtube.com and type the following into their search field: "Early morning madness with Scout the Fennec Fox"

- A very hyper Fennec – This video shows a hyper fennec fox releasing some energy.

If unable to access the above link, go to youtube.com and type the following into their search field: "Fennecs are absolutely crazy"

- Fennec and a Cat – This is a video of a fennec and a cat playing and enjoying each other's company.

If unable to access the above link, go to youtube.com and type the following into their search field: "Fennec Fox and Cat Playing"

Final Thoughts

So, do fennec foxes make good pets? Well, I think the more important question is would you make a good fennec fox pet owner?

If you fully understand and accept the responsibilities of caring for such a special and exotic pet, then you may be prepared to call a cute little fennec your own. However, if you find the responsibilities to be too much or to be overwhelming, then that's ok too. These cute little creatures aren't for everyone. The important thing is that you do your research before making a decision.

Whatever decision you make, please do so with the animal in mind. It is unfair to take on any type of pet ownership without being fully prepared to meet all of the pet's needs. You should purchase your fennec, or any pet, with the goal to provide it with the best home possible.

These animals require time, energy, understanding, and patience. But they also provide great enjoyment and pleasure to those who love them.

I hope this book helps you to make the best decision possible.

All the best,

Julie

Notes

CPSIA information can be obtained at www.ICGtesting.com
Printed in the USA
LVOW01s0315140814

399091LV00010B/131/P